BRONKS and Richard Jordan Productions
with Theatre Royal Plymouth and Big in Belgium
in association with Summerhall

US/THEM

by Carly Wijs

Us/Them premiered in Dutch at BRONKS Theatre in Brussels
on 27 September, 2014.

The production received its UK premiere in English at Summerhall
as part of the Edinburgh Festival Fringe on 3 August 2016.

It subsequently transferred to the Dorfman auditorium of the
National Theatre, London, on 16 January 2017.

The production was produced by BRONKS and Richard Jordan Productions
with Theatre Royal Plymouth and Big in Belgium in association with Summerhall
It was directed by Carly Wijs.

BRONKS | Richard Jordan Productions Ltd

TRP | THEATRE ROYAL PLYMOUTH

The author received a grant from the Flemish Literature Fund for the writing of this piece.

US/THEM

by Carly Wijs

Cast

Gytha Parmentier
Roman Van Houtven

Creative Team

Director	Carly Wijs
Created with	Thomas Vantuycom
Designer	Stef Stessel
Lighting Design	Thomas Clause
Sound Design	Peter Brughmans
Dramaturg	Mieke Versyp

BRONKS and Richard Jordan Productions
with Theatre Royal Plymouth and Big in Belgium
in association with Summerhall

Biographies

CARLY WIJS (Writer) has written and created plays, and has performed as a film and theatre actress with Wim Vandekeybus/Ultima Vez, Guy Cassiers, Josse De Pauw, De Roovers, KOPERGIETERY, Muziektheater Transparant et al. Her productions have toured internationally. She is regularly invited to be a guest lecturer at the RITS and P.A.R.T.S. (both in Brussels). Her first novel *The Doubtexperiment* was published in May 2016 and nominated for the Flemish debut prize: The Bronze Owl. *Us/Them* won her an Edinburgh Fringe First at the 2016 Festival.

GYTHA PARMENTIER (Performer) recently graduated from the KASK in Ghent and has previously worked as an actress with het KIP, Luxemburg vzw and Alain Platel.

ROMAN VAN HOUTVEN (Performer) graduated from the P.A.R.T.S. dance school. During and after his studies, he worked on projects with fABULEUS, Impuls Company, Dancingkids (Rosas Education), DE studio, Galacticamendum and Daniel Linehan/Hiatus. In association with BRONKS, De Munt and Q-O2 he choreographed the music theatre production *Frankenstein*.

STEF STESSEL (Designer) has worked as a designer on several theatre productions by HETPALEIS, de Roovers, Toneelhuis and other companies.

MIEKE VERSYP (Dramaturg) has previously worked with Carly as a dramaturg on the production *The daddy, the mummy and the Nazi…* (KOPERGIETERY), as well as with Studio Orka and Ontroerend Goed. She has also written several children's books (Linus, Soepletters, et al.).

 **THEATRE
ROYAL
PLYMOUTH**

THEATRE ROYAL PLYMOUTH is the largest and best attended regional producing theatre in the UK and the leading promoter of theatre in the South West. We produce and present a broad range of theatre in our three distinctive performance spaces – The Lyric, The Drum and The Lab – including classic and contemporary drama, musicals, opera, ballet and dance. We specialise in the production of new plays and have built a national reputation for the quality and innovation of our programme. Our extensive creative-learning work is pioneering and engages young people and communities in Plymouth and beyond. Our award-winning waterfront Production and Learning centre,TR2, is a unique building with unrivalled set, costume, prop-making and rehearsal facilities. Recent Theatre Royal Plymouth productions include: *Monster Raving Loony* by James Graham, *The Man with the Hammer* by Phil Porter, *The Whipping Man* by Matthew Lopez, *After Electra* by April de Angelis, *Grand Guignol and Horse Piss for Blood* by Carl Grose, *Merit* by Alexandra Wood, *Another Place* by DC Moore, *Chekhov in Hell* by Dan Rebellato, *The Astronaut's Chair* by Rona Munro, *Solid Air* by Doug Lucie, and *MADMAN* by Chris Goode. The Theatre Royal Plymouth also collaborates with some of the best artists and theatremakers in the UK and internationally. We have regularly co-produced with Ontroerend Goed and Richard Jordan Productions (*World Without Us*, *Are we not drawn onward to new erA*, *A History of Everything*, *Sirens*, *Fight Night*), Paines Plough (*The Angry Brigade* by James Graham, *Love Love Love* by Mike Bartlett), Frantic Assembly (*Othello*, *The Believers* by Bryony Lavery, *Lovesong* by Abi Morgan) and Told By An Idiot (*Heads Will Roll*, *My Perfect Mind*, *And The Horse You Rode In On*). We have also co-produced with Complicite (*The Master and Margarita*, *A Disappearing Number*), Hofesh Shechter (*Sun*, *Political Mother*), Graeae (*The Solid Life of Sugar Water*) and David Pugh, Dafydd Rogers, Kneehigh Theatre (*Rebecca*) and Jamie Hendry Productions (*The Wind in the Willows*). Alongside our own productions we present a programme of quality and popularity and regularly launch national touring productions including *Swan Lake* and *Edward Scissorhands* (Matthew Bourne), *War Horse* (National Theatre) and most recently *Billy Elliot the Musical*.

For the Theatre Royal Plymouth

Chief Executive	Adrian Vinken OBE
Artistic Director	Simon Stokes
Executive Producer	Victoria Allen
Marketing & Communications Director	Marianne Locatori
Operations Director	Helen Costello

Summerhall

SUMMERHALL presents engaging, challenging and exhilarating visual arts, theatre, dance, music, literature and education for people of all ages in the unique buildings of Edinburgh's former Royal (Dick) Veterinary College. We host diverse programmes of visual and performance art throughout the year as well as events, parties, other festivals, workshops – even weddings. Summerhall provides workspaces for artists, innovators and community organisations as well as encouraging the creation and application of new technologies in our high tech hub – the TechCube. Summerhall is for everyone. Whether you are engaging with our exhibitions, catching the best in avant-garde European theatre, grabbing something to drink in the Royal Dick bar or simply soaking up the atmosphere in our buzzy courtyard, there is something for you to explore, discover and most of all, enjoy, this Festival and all year round.

Big in Belgium

Now in its fourth year, **BIG IN BELGIUM** provides a platform for Flemish theatre during the Edinburgh Festival Fringe. Every year a selection of Flemish plays are translated into English and presented, aiming to create a greater visibility for Flemish theatre on the international scene.

BRONKS

BRONKS is a Brussels-based art house with an accent on theatre for a young audience. The artistic guidance is in the hands of Veerle Kerckhoven and Marij De Nys. BRONKS aims with its artistic and art education activities to stimulate children, youth and their environment to discover and explore the possibilities in ourselves and in the world.

Each season, BRONKS invites several artists to make a production for children or youth. This results in three inhouse productions per year, presented not only in the BRONKS theatre, but also on tour. A new theatre text is written for many BRONKS creations. By offering both starting theatre-makers and established names and artists from other disciplines the opportunity to create their first performance for children, BRONKS aims to generate enthusiasm for the performing arts for a young audience. In addition to its own work, BRONKS also presents guest productions from beginning and experienced companies and makers from Flanders, the Netherlands and sometimes from other countries. Moreover, BRONKS focuses not only on theatre, but also on music, dance, the visual arts and film.

BRONKS has developed extensive educational activities for schools as well as for children and youth who wish to pursue the performing arts in their free time. Students and teachers can come to BRONKS for school performances, introductions, post-performance discussions, workshops and long-term theatre projects. Via STUDIO BRONKS, the house organises workshops outside school hours in which children and youth can actively explore the theatre medium.

Richard Jordan
Productions Ltd

RICHARD JORDAN PRODUCTIONS is an Olivier and TONY Award-winning production company based in London under the artistic leadership of British producer Richard Jordan. Founded in 1998, his company has produced over 205 productions in the UK as well as 24 other countries, including 75 world premieres and 81 European, Australian or US premieres producing and collaborating with many of the world's leading theatres. Described by *The Stage* newspaper as 'one of the UK's most prolific theatre producers', Richard Jordan Productions has been at the forefront of developing and/or commissioning works often with a strong social and political agenda. The company has produced a diverse range of established and emerging writers and artists from around the world including: Conor McPherson; Omphile Molusi; Alan Bennett; Cora Bissett; Athol Fugard; David Greig; Martin McDonagh; Alan Ayckbourn; Karla Crome; Valentijn Dhaenens; Danai Gurira; Nikkole Salter; Charlotte Josephine; Ben Brown; Cristian Ceresoli; Luke Barnes; Christopher Durang; Nick Steur; Stephen Sondheim; Robert Farquhar; the Q Brothers; one step at a time like this; Mike Cullen; Charles Hart; Heather Raffo and Stefan Golaszewski. A new-writing specialist, Richard served for seven years as an Associate Artist of London's Bush Theatre, and as Creative Director of London's Theatre Royal Haymarket and Artistic Consultant for the creation and inaugural season of the Theatre Royal Haymarket Company. He is the international Producing Partner of Chicago Shakespeare Theater and the Illawarra Performing Arts Centre (IPAC) in Wollongong, Australia.

Richard has enjoyed a long association with Belgium, producing and developing the work of some of its country's most exciting new and leading contemporary artists and companies which began in 2008 with the Belgian collective Ontroerend Goed whose work he co-produces worldwide. In 2012, he co-created and produces Big in Belgium which hosts an annual selection of Belgian productions at the Edinburgh Fringe. Over the past four years, it has established itself as a major international season of contemporary works winning a variety of awards and has enjoyed wide critical success. Richard's past productions have won over 40 major awards including: the TONY Award for Best Play; Olivier Award for Outstanding Achievement at an Affiliate Theatre; Emmy Award for Best Feature Section; 14 Scotsman Fringe Firsts Awards; 3 Herald Angel Awards; 9 Total Theatre Awards; Amnesty International Freedom of Expression Award; Spirit of the Fringe Award; Off-West End Award for Best Musical; 3 Helen Hayes Awards; Adelaide Festival Award; US Black Alliance Award; Stage Award; Obie Award; John Gassner Award for Best New American Play; Jeff Award; Lucille Lortel Award and the Drama Desk, Drama League, New York Critics and Outer Critic Circle Best New Play Awards. In 1998 as the first recipient of the Society of London Theatre/TIF New Producers Bursary Award, Richard left working for the National Theatre to form his own production company.

For more information, please contact:
Richard Jordan Productions, Mews Studios, 16 Vernon Yard, London W11 2DX, United Kingdom, +44 (0) 207 243 9001, info@richardjordanproductions.com

US/THEM

Carly Wijs

Introduction
Carly Wijs

BRONKS are a theatre company for young audiences based in Brussels, Belgium. When they asked me if I was interested in creating a performance for them, in 2013, the terrorist attack in a shopping mall in Nairobi, Kenya, had just occurred. I had read about it in the newspapers and watched footage of it on television, but I had not discussed it with my then eight-year-old son.

But he had seen it for himself on the news and he came to tell me. The way he talked about the attack was very specific: objective, aloof, with the ability to overlook the emotional implications. He handled the news factually, as a sequence of events, and without having to connect it to a judgement. It was as if the horror for him as an eight-year-old child had a completely different meaning because it was not possible to relate it to his own life. A child, unlike an adult, does not think: 'That could have been me.'

I started to think about another horrifying act of unspeakable violence – the Beslan school siege of September 2004 – and how this dark episode in history could combine with the thoughts and impressions of children about such acts, to make a piece of theatre for young people. I subsequently managed to persuade Oda Van Neygen, who was at the time artistic director of BRONKS, and to this day I thank her for her courage in allowing me do it.

If you type 'Beslan' into Google and look at the pictures, it is riveting. You cannot let go of the horror. The fact that it involves children makes that feeling even stronger. It is an abomination in the extreme. But how can we put such indescribable acts on stage? How can we make something that is totally incomprehensible, understandable? And isn't it taboo to make a piece of theatre about terrorism, aimed at audiences of children? Ultimately, I do not believe it is taboo – in fact, no subject should be taboo for children. It is just important that you use the right words. Discussing the topic of terrorism with children is a challenge, but it can be done. And *must* be done.

Why Beslan? Well, the drama took place at a school, and the first day of school is something to which every child can relate. The fact that the terrorists chose that specific day and environment to stage their atrocity reflects a profound perversion – but I did not want to talk about the perversity of it all. That's just an ongoing debate by adults: why is this happening? A child cannot answer and does not have to answer that question. That is the privilege of being a child.

Whilst doing research, I came across a gripping BBC documentary called *Children of Beslan*, in which the story of the siege is told by the children who were held hostage (it's available to watch on YouTube). These children gave the same factual account of those events as my son had given about the Nairobi attack. Aloof almost. Which, of course, does not mean that these children do not have an enormous trauma to process. Unfortunately, the horrifying implications of what happened to them will probably hit them when they grow up. But the only thing that seemed to count for the children in the documentary was that the story was told as *accurately* as possible.

It was because of this documentary that I decided to tell the story entirely from the perspective of the children involved: one boy and one girl. There is a difference between their perspectives, but they both try to be as precise as possible in their accounts of what happened during the three-day siege. This precision sometimes takes the form of a 'Show and Tell' presentation, a scientific paper or a maths lesson, like you get in school…

But sometimes the children flee from the horror, straight into the comforting arms of the imagination. In the documentary, a boy fantasised that Harry Potter would arrive wearing his invisibility cloak and kill the terrorists one by one. Others fantasised that they were part of a film and none of this was really happening to them. In the play, the children devise their own endings to the siege that are either extremely happy or extremely sad.

Almost 1,200 people, including 777 children, were held hostage during the siege. Outside the school there must have been several thousand people. And yet, in the news footage, Google searches and documentaries, you keep seeing the same group of about fifty photogenic people. In all of the footage that has survived from those fateful days, it's always the scenes of greatest desperation and devastation that play on a loop, that come back time and time again. Even though the story – and other stories like it – need no further dramatisation, the media keep pushing that sentimental 'drama' button. And we keep watching.

This manipulation of our feelings, and the fact we allow it to happen, is neither innocent, or inconsequential. If – or *when* – we are blinded and overwhelmed by emotions, we stop being able to think and reflect and analyse. Our only response becomes 'Oh my god, this is terrible.' And yet it is essential that we don't stop thinking and reflecting and analysing. Only by doing so can we get to the origins of these atrocities – and then, we hope, start to think about preventing them.

As adults, we are conditioned by our overly dramatised perspective, by the media, by ourselves, into black and white thinking: 'Us' versus 'Them'. The refreshing thing about a child's gaze is that it is not coloured by the need for 'dramatic interpretation', because that view of things does not connect to their own life. And if it does connect to their own life, it is tackled through imagination. That is what *Us/Them* is about.

Characters

GIRL
BOY

An empty stage. At the back there is a wall or blackboard with coat hooks sticking out of it.

On the floor in front of the blackboard there are two pieces of chalk and a sponge. To the right of the stage, a bunch of black helium balloons, held down by a large block of wood. A BOY and a GIRL appear. They walk past the balloons and each take a piece of chalk. Then they walk to the front of the stage and begin to draw lines on the floor. Although they start at the same spot, there is soon a clear difference between their two drawings.

GIRL *and* BOY. These are the outbuildings. That's where the toddlers are.

While the GIRL is drawing, she constantly mumbles measurements to herself and checks whether they match what she is drawing on the floor. She looks irritated at the BOY who is drawing a different-sized plan. In turn, the BOY is annoyed with the GIRL because she is getting in his way.

This is the gymnasium.
Adjoining it is the large main building.
There are three floors.
The main building towers over the other buildings.
From here you can see the whole terrain.
There are twenty classrooms spread over three floors. On the ground floor to the right is a canteen.

They have finished drawing. On the floor we see two versions of the school plan drawn over each other in chalk, overlapping in places. The BOY and the GIRL explain the layout of the buildings, pointing out the various locations. But as their drawings and stories are not exactly the same, they point in different directions. Sometimes they complement each other, sometimes they contradict each other, and sometimes they try to outpace the other.

On the third floor the offices of the director and the administration.

They each point out a different place for the library.

And a library with two thousand eight hundred and seventy-nine books. Mainly textbooks, but also five hundred and thirty-three children's books with stories.
Surrounding the buildings, a large play area in a U-shape. There are three entries or exits.

In front of the main building, on the left, the main entrance. On the right side a side entrance. Very practical: if you are late for school, you can sneak in and join the rows.
In between the main building and the first extension is another exit. This exit is very useful: in case of a fire, people can escape in all directions.

In case of danger, you only have to barricade three doors.
Next to the canteen is a small kitchen. That's where they make the soup and the potatoes that we eat for lunch. On the other side of the kitchen is a staircase. That leads to a hidden cellar. That basement cannot be seen from the outside, but also not from the kitchen.
At the front of the building is the small town. The school is the largest in the town.

BOY. According to many people also the best school.

GIRL. It's School Number One.

The following summary of facts is completely rattled off with accompanying gestures.

BOY *and* GIRL. The town has approximately thirty-three thousand six hundred and forty-six people.
Three swimming pools.
One Museum of Folk Art.
Twenty-one churches.
Fifty-three mosques.
Five tennis courts.
Seven parks, most of which without ponds and ducks.
One hundred and four baker's.

Forty-eight butcher's.

Twelve supermarkets, three of which are very large.

Five thousand registered cats.

Eight thousand six hundred and twenty-four chickens that lay forty-two thousand one hundred and twenty eggs per week.

Four vegetarians.

Two hospitals, three hundred nurses. Fifty-eight doctors.

Three police stations with fifteen policemen. Nothing much happens here.

The GIRL walks forward and points at a spot behind the audience.

GIRL. Behind the school there's a forest. There's a path from the school that leads straight through the forest to the border.

GIRL *and* BOY. A hundred and twenty kilometres away.

GIRL. On the other side of the border is Chechnya, with its capital Grozny.

There the children can only go to school until they are eight. Then they must work.

Mostly in brothels for paedophiles.

The fathers are addicted to drugs.

The mothers all have moustaches and have to work like horses.

There are no tennis courts.

BOY. No, no tennis courts.

The BOY walks to the back and tries to get the GIRL to go with him, but she wants to tell us more about Chechnya. He goes and draws a large rectangle in chalk on the right side of the stage. Round the bunch of balloons. Then he sees that, in her enthusiasm, the GIRL has erased his version of the gymnasium with her foot. Angrily he walks to the spot and carefully redraws the lines that she has erased.

GIRL. When you enter Chechnya from the border, the forest changes into boring fields. But on our side it is stunning. Really marvellous. A paradise-like nature. In a well-known hiking guide for professional hikers this path has been described as:

BOY. 'The most beautiful trail in the region, with magnificent views.'

GIRL. You'll see the white-headed duck, the black vulture, the Caucasian salamander, but also lots of wild sheep, which are known for their long woollen fleece. As a child I used to lay on one. They are very popular all over the world.

The GIRL *shuffles over towards the spot where the* BOY *is at the balloons.*

BOY (*indicating the chalk rectangle he has just drawn*). Here is a podium.

GIRL *and* BOY. That's where the principal and thirty-five teachers are.
To the right of the podium are rows of parents, about five hundred and three in total.

Three hundred and seventy-eight mothers, one hundred and three grandmothers and twenty-two fathers.
In the middle of the playground the children are arranged in rows.

A total of seven hundred and fifty, aged two-and-a-half to twelve years.
They each have seven balloons in their hands, one for each year that they are in school. That is a total of five thousand two hundred and fifty balloons.

GIRL. It is the largest school in the region.

BOY. You already said that.

BOY *and* GIRL. On the left side of the stage, is a choir of twenty children. They have been selected to sing some songs on this day.
The first song is called 'Oh Wonderful New Future'.

They sing the song and perform choreographed movements – the kind that would help children to remember the words of a song.

O wonderful new future
I beg you, to have mercy
I beg you, please have mercy
Have mercy on me
Today's a new beginning
Of a wonderful new future
My wonderful new future
I run into your arms.

GIRL. Masha also sings in the choir.

BOY. The second song is called 'In the Fields' and it goes
like this…

*The BOY begins to sing 'Poljushko Polje' by Lev Knipper
and Viktor Gusev, but is interrupted by the GIRL, who runs
forward again and starts talking about Masha.*

GIRL. I want to tell you anyway.
What happened to Masha… a really terrible story…
Last year a disaster occurred on September 1st. The first
school day was a catastrophe. Because of the heat, it is hot
now, but last year it was, thirty-two degrees Celsius in the
shade on September 1st, and Masha fainted. Just like that.
Boom. Flat out on the floor. Terrible. Her eyes turned away.
Completely dehydrated. So this year all the children and
parents were given a bottle of water at the entrance. At all
costs last year's drama had to be avoided.
That is why this year we start at nine instead of ten o'clock.
It's only twenty-three degrees at that time.

BOY. The second song is called 'In the Fields' and it goes
like this…

He sings two bars but is interrupted by the GIRL again.

GIRL. Helmut Lotti made a very beautiful version.

*Helmut Lotti's version of 'Poljushko Polje' plays. The BOY
listens, annoyed, but still sings along. The GIRL enjoys the
beautiful sound of Helmut's voice.*

Then the mood changes. The song continues, but the GIRL *and the* BOY *start to speak, hurried and urgent. Their voices are hardly audible over the loud music, but we can hear words, snatches of what happened during the terrorists' raid of the school.*

GIRL *and* BOY. The terrorists come from over there.
From the dark forest.
A group of thirty-five storm the school.
They wear masks and guns.
Immediately they occupy the three entrances of the school.
In the schoolyard the festivities continue.
The choir sings on.
People think it's the balloons that pop.
It's only when Masha starts her solo that everyone sees the terrorists and the children let go of their balloons.
People flee into the main building.
A small group runs to the boiler room.
In the main building the exits are blocked.
Everyone is looking for shelter.
A boy hid in a cupboard, while he heard the rest go by.
Here a girl crawled on to a rack, with coats spread over her.
Someone stood behind the curtain, but her feet were still visible, so she got caught.

GIRL (*simultaneous*). A teacher pushed as many parents and children as possible into the cellar, until she was taken away by one of the terrorists and brought to the gymnasium through the small corridor. The people that were left in the cellar escaped during the night.
In the gymnasium: one thousand one hundred and forty-eight people. The terrorists surrounding them are heavily armed. They were ordered to sit down, all of them, with their hands on their head.
In the meantime, in the boiler room, the escaped people crawled over, along, under, behind… the machines, to the other side.

BOY (*simultaneous*). Meanwhile, the people in the boiler room were crawling under the pipes and over the pipes.

Children were passed on.

Towels, that were placed there to dry, were hanging over the pipes.

I participated in the regional school basketball tournament and that was the week before, so plenty of towels were used. We came first in the tournament and I scored five points.

The towels were used to cover the pipes, so no one got burned by the pipes.

BOY *and* GIRL. It was very warm.

Eventually they were able to jump out of the window.

GIRL (*simultaneous*). In the gymnasium, the men were pointed out one by one and taken. We could hear them walking down the corridor, up the stairs, past the first classroom, the second class, the third, past the library, and into the sixth grade. In that room there was an argument between a female terrorist and the leader of the terrorists. She had a bomb vest, he had the button. By detonating her, four of the men died. They were thrown out of the window. The others had to stand by the window and one by one they were shot. They toppled over the railings and fell to the other side...

BOY (*simultaneous*). Meanwhile, next to the stage, Masha had come round.

Her leg was bleeding, but her new dress, which had cost three hundred roubles, was still intact.

She tried to very quietly crawl across the floor in the direction of the exit to the right of the school and had to halt during a hail of bullets.

In the second annexe two children were waiting to escape, but they could not get away.

On the side of the podium terrorists ran back and forth to drive the last people inside.

Masha crawled back further towards the exit and eventually came upon a group of men who had been thrown out the window... and were lying...

The music stops.

GIRL *and* BOY....Dead on the playground.

The BOY *and* GIRL *start to breathe with difficulty; they rattle and seem to choke.*

That's not the sound of those dying men.

BOY. Not the sound of Masha. She keeps quiet and pretends she's dead.
That's the sound of one thousand one hundred and forty-eight people in the gymnasium that dehydrate.

GIRL *and* BOY *simultaneously move their bodies in various corresponding poses, acting out what they describe.*

BOY *and* GIRL. First, the saliva disappears from your mouth.
You get a dry throat.
You get a headache.
You stop peeing.

You become nauseous.
You get cramps.
Your whole body tingles.
You get cold hands and feet.
Your nails turn blue.
Your consciousness decreases.
Pretty soon you'll get confused.
And that is exactly where you want to be.
A pure hallucination.

BOY. Sausages fall from heaven.
Delicious sausages.
Tomatoes are shot down with big tomato bazookas.
Sausages in tomato sauce.

GIRL. There is a tree and shadow.
Aerial roots from the tree.
Between the aerial roots a giraffe with long legs dances in the air.
On the horizon there's a little stream flowing your way, closer and closer.
You put your lips to the stream and if you drink, pee no longer tastes bad.

BOY. Sausages in tomato sauce with a glass of lovely lukewarm pee…

BOY *and* GIRL. However, that is only at the end of the second day. On the first day at nine twenty-eight the door of the gymnasium is barricaded. Nobody can get out. One thousand one hundred and forty-eight people are trapped in the gymnasium. When everyone is inside, terrorists start placing wires across the room.

The GIRL *and* BOY *walk to the blackboard at the back and pull out the coat hooks. They are attached to long ropes. The* GIRL *and* BOY *stretch the ropes out across the room, tightening them like wires. The room gets wired up until there is barely enough space to stand or move.*

GIRL (*as she tightens the wire*). You don't have to be afraid. There are three hundred and fifty-six fathers who have gone to work on September 1st and who are not in the gymnasium. The fathers will all come immediately when they hear what has happened. One of the fathers has the fastest tractor in the region! The first bullets were at…?

BOY. Seven past nine.

GIRL. Exactly. At seven past nine the father with the fastest tractor in the region will have just finished the first potato field! He harvested a lot of potatoes this year. Mash is delicious and very nutritious. He is very strong thanks to all those potatoes.

BOY. Another father is the best butcher in town. His shop is located three kilometres away. When the first shot is fired, at nine oh seven, he hears nothing. He will be carefully cutting a purple-red fillet from the carcass of a cow. That brings in a lot of money. Meat is the most important part of our diet. A fillet of one hundred grams has enough protein for the whole week. Potatoes don't have that at all.

GIRL. The father with the tractor has a mobile phone that will ring at ten minutes past nine. He will be told that there is shooting at our school, immediately drop the potatoes, turn his tractor with all his might and go full speed. While the father in the butcher's is still quietly cutting into the meat, the father with the tractor will already be on his way.

BOY. The father in the butcher shop does not need a mobile phone, because at fifteen minutes past nine Grigori will rush to the butchery: 'Eh-eh-ah-he' – the father who has just finished cutting the fillet will strike Grigori in the face, to stop his stuttering. Grigori is a bit simple. But reliable and he knows everything that goes on in our town. Grigori will talk about shots at school number one. 'S-S-S-Siege.' The father will immediately storm on to the street. Knife in the left, axe in his right hand and Grigori behind him. The father jumps in front of the first car that comes along. 'To School Number One.' He will call out. 'There is a shooting!' The driver of the car will also be a father and the three of them will immediately drive to the school.

GIRL. The other father will drive his tractor on to the highway. That's not allowed, but he doesn't care. Smoke will come out of his engine, but he will not see this, because he will only think of his wife and child whom he has to save. There's really no need to be afraid.
The tractor will overtake everyone. The cars honking, but he will shout: 'The terrorists have come to School Number One!' The people who honked will also start to drive fast, because they are also fathers and like an army of fathers they will race to the school.

BOY. They will arrive at the school with sliding tyres. The butcher, the driver of the car and Grigori followed by police officers, firefighters, veterinarians. All fathers. The butcher will take the lead and, while zigzagging, run to the side entrance. Bullets will whistle past his ears, but he is not afraid. He went to school here, so he knows the building like his back pocket.

GIRL. The tractor will stop by the hospital to pick up two doctors who are smoking outside. They hang on to the tractor and call out: 'Our children are in that school. Can't you go any faster!!?' And yes he can. The tractor will fly forward with a jerk!

BOY. A few metres before the entrance of the school, the butcher stumbles and loses his shoe. Grigori follows with

two bricks in his hands. He calls 'S-S-S-SHOE!' The father
from the butcher shop will hesitate, there's glass everywhere.

GIRL. While the butcher is hesitating over a shoe, the tractor
drives past at full speed followed by twenty cars full of
fathers. The tractor will drive round the school to the back
where the forest begins.

BOY. The father from the best butcher shop in town will only
hesitate for one second and then he walks straight through
the glass to the side entrance. There he sees a mother who
has escaped and therefore is not in the gymnasium. It is his
wife and she will throw her arms around his neck while she
cries: 'Our son, our son is inside... Oh, do something.'
The butcher's wife is always very emotional. That is
embarrassing. The butcher will feel a brief shudder go
through his body, but he will not cry. He is a husband and
a father, and he has an axe in one hand and a knife in the
other hand.

GIRL. At the back of the school the father gives the tractor full
throttle – HENG, heeeng! – but he will keep the parking
brake on. At the right time he will let go of the brake and
drive into the left corner of the gymnasium straight through
the reinforced concrete. Somewhere over here...
When he gets the nine ten phone call, he will be on the
motorway by nine thirteen. Seven minutes later he arrives at
the hospital, and it takes another seven minutes to get to
town. Past the church, past the Museum of Folk Art... He is
here at nine thirty-one.

All the wires have now been strung and the BOY *goes to
stand at the back of the gymnasium. The* GIRL *goes to stand
with him. They wait for the tractor. It doesn't come.*

Perhaps one of the doctors couldn't find his medical bag and
the tractor had to wait... So then within one minute...
Or he had a red light in Church Street. That takes fifteen
seconds at least!...
But if you have a red light there, you also have a red light at
the next intersection. So another twenty seconds...

GIRL *and* BOY. One… two… three… four… five… six… seven… eight…

GIRL. That's a little fast. You should count slowly: nine ten bread and butter…

GIRL *and* BOY. Eleven bread and butter twelve bread and butter thirteen bread and butter…

BOY. No, that is too slow. Fourteen… fifteen…

GIRL *and* BOY. Sixteen… seventeen…

BOY. Seventeen and a half…

GIRL *and* BOY. Eight…

Nobody comes. They slowly raise their arms in the air. They are caught in a tangle of wires.

BOY. We are not allowed to play.

GIRL. We are not allowed to speak.

BOY. We are not allowed to lower our hands.
We are not allowed to pee.

GIRL. That is not true.

BOY. We are not allowed to do a poo.

GIRL. We can pee and poo, we are not allowed to use the toilet.

BOY. We are not allowed to open a window.

GIRL. We cannot drink.
We can eat the flowers we brought for the teacher.

BOY. We cannot use the mobile phone.

GIRL. We cannot read.

BOY. Not sit together.

GIRL. Not drink.

BOY. Not play with the ball.

GIRL. No lava floor.

BOY. Not go outside.

GIRL. Snitch.
Drink.

BOY. We are not allowed to pick our nose.

GIRL. Sit with Mummy.

BOY. We are never allowed to pick our nose.

GIRL. Cry.

BOY. Drink.

GIRL. Ask questions.

BOY. Complain.
Look directly into eyes.

GIRL. Drink.
Giraffe.

The BOY *laughs.*

Drink.

BOY *and* GIRL. Stink.

BOY. Basket hoop.

GIRL. Stinkempoop.

BOY. Protest.

GIRL. Breast.

The BOY *runs away from the* GIRL *and sits down on the floor on the other side of the room with his hands in the air.*

BOY. There are children in the room. You and your breasts…

GIRL (*mumbling while taking off her skirt*). It is very hot in here. I'm going to tell him that he can also take something off.

She carefully walks towards the BOY. *He has his head turned away from her. Slowly, the music of 'Oh Wonderful New Future' begins to play. She pulls his jersey up. He pulls it back down. She tries again and ends up sitting on his lap in her underwear. They sing along to the chorus of 'Oh Wonderful New Future'. As the music plays they begin to move around. Initially because the* BOY *is trying to get rid of the* GIRL, *but soon it becomes a game where they have move through the space as much as possible without touching the wires. As they continue to play they become overconfident and brush against the wires, which begin to move dangerously. Startled, they shrink back. The music stops abruptly. There is silence. The* BOY *starts to explain what the wires really are.*

BOY. Bombs.

GIRL. The terrorists hang bombs in the gymnasium. These bombs are connected by wires. Those wires hang like garlands around the gymnasium.

BOY. Making bombs is a lot of work. It takes hours.

GIRL. You need to connect the correct wires.
Make no mistakes.

The BOY *and the* GIRL *collect some of the balloons from the right side of the stage and tie them to the wires around the stage.*

BOY. You are surrounded by one thousand one hundred and forty-eight whining people with their hands in the air.

GIRL. One thousand one hundred and forty-six.

BOY. Why one thousand one hundred and forty-six?

GIRL. First there were one thousand one hundred and forty-eight, but then only one thousand one hundred and forty-six.

The BOY *is silent as he lets go of a bad memory in his head.*

BOY. Oh yeah….
One thousand one hundred and forty-six people are crammed into the gymnasium.
They moan.
They sigh.
They talk.

They make a lot of noise.
Yet the terrorist must connect the wires correctly.
That takes hours.
And it is getting warmer.

GIRL. Bombs are hanging from the basket hoop.
In between there are wires.
A bomb in the middle with a wire down to the detonator.

BOY. On the detonator a book.
On the book a foot.

He puts his foot on the big wooden block.

Attached to the foot –
a terrorist.

The GIRL *carefully walks forward and whispers to the audience.*

GIRL. The terrorist must be still.
He cannot move.
Not scratch when it itches.
Not think about breasts.

The BOY *cannot keep a straight face and giggles very loudly.*

No cramp.
No fainting.

BOY. The foot is changed every two hours.
This is a very precise work.
Two terrorists each hold the book down with their hands.

GIRL. I will pretend to be two terrorists.
The pressure of the hands must be exactly the same as the
pressure of the foot.

She puts her hands on the block next to the BOY*'s foot.*

BOY. No more and no less.
Then the terrorist very carefully removes his foot.

GIRL. The four hands are now the foot.
Then a fourth terrorist very carefully places his foot on
the book.

BOY. He breathes, looks straight ahead and nods.
  Then the kneeling terrorists carefully let go of the book.

GIRL. After two hours, the same again.

BOY. After two hours again.

GIRL. All day and all night.

BOY. Every two hours the same movement.

  While the BOY *recites the following lines the* GIRL *jumps in the air as if she's exploding. The explosions get larger with each line.*

  You cannot wiggle your toes.
  You cannot play some basketball.
  You cannot do like this.
  You cannot go to a friend across the hall. 'Hey John...'
  You cannot stretch.
  You cannot think about the meaning of life.
  You cannot explain why you're here.

GIRL. Why are we here?

BOY. Why are we in the gymnasium with one thousand one hundred and forty-one people.

GIRL. Because they are paedophiles?

BOY. Because their mothers have a moustache.

GIRL. What is that?

BOY. That is hair on your upper lip.

GIRL. I know that.

BOY. Then why do you ask?

GIRL. What is a paedophile?

BOY. Don't you know that?

GIRL. Yes.

BOY. Not.

GIRL. I do.

BOY. Not.

GIRL. What is it then?

The BOY *cannot answer her.*

Ha!

She walks over to the wall and starts to count.

If it had been a normal second school day, we would start with maths.

The BOY *cheerfully jumps up and rushes to the blackboard.*

BOY. Calculations.

GIRL (*disappointed*). I'm no good at calculations.

BOY. Imagine: you have thirty-five terrorists. Thirty-three men and two women.
And one thousand one hundred and forty people in the gymnasium.

GIRL. One thousand one hundred and thirty-nine.

BOY. One thousand one hundred and thirty-nine people in the gymnasium.
If every terrorist holds the same number of people at gunpoint, how many do they each keep at gunpoint?
Remember they detonated two women because they gave the children water.

GIRL (*to the audience*). Their face was covered by a veil. We are not sure if they had a moustache.
(*To the* BOY.) I think you are saying it in a very complicated way.

BOY. You have to do that; a calculation is always complicated.

GIRL. If the two female terrorists have exploded then there are just thirty-three terrorists and then you divide one thousand one hundred and thirty-nine by thirty-three.

BOY. One thousand one hundred and thirty-eight.

GIRL. No, not yet…

BOY. That is… let me think… let me think… let me think…

He calculates on the blackboard.

One thousand one hundred and thirty-nine divided by thirty-three equals thirty-four point five one five one five one.

GIRL. Rather a lot per terrorist.

BOY. Remember that the terrorist who has his foot on the bomb cannot keep anyone at gunpoint.

GIRL. Of course. So it is one thousand one hundred and thirty-nine divided by thirty-two.

BOY. No, no no… not really…

The GIRL *sighs.*

There is something else.
The terrorists are here because they want something…

He starts writing on the blackboard. At the top of his list, he writes: 'deemands'. Language is clearly not his thing…

They have demands.
There are six:
One – a free and independent Chechnya.
Two – free Chechnya of occupying troops.
Three – a free retreat for the terrorists.
Four – peace.
Five – freedom of religion.
Six – free all political prisoners.

The GIRL *sees the spelling mistake and giggles. The* BOY *writes a shortened version of the demands on the board. When he's finished, there is the following list:*

1– Free
2 – Free
3 – Free
4 – Peace
5 – Free
6 – Free

GIRL. I don't understand.

BOY. What don't you understand? Po-li-ti-cal prisoners?

GIRL. I don't understand the demands. Why do they want this
from me? I have five rouble in my piggy bank. They can
have that. I also have ten Barbies. That's a lot and I don't
mind giving them away. But I have no army and no troops
and no political prisoners.
What are they again?

BOY. Phew, don't you even know that...?

GIRL (*angrily*). I know nothing about Chechnya. Except about
the paedophiles and the moustaches.

BOY. So it is one thousand one hundred and thirty-nine divided
by thirty-two if we exclude the terrorist with his foot on the
detonator.
But if we can please a few terrorists with five roubles and ten
Barbies then there might be a few less.

GIRL. The women might like to have the Barbies.

BOY. They no longer count. They have exploded. The men
don't want a Barbie. Terrorists do not play with Barbie.

GIRL. And the roubles?

BOY. Five roubles divided by thirty-two is... oh no... maybe
the terrorist with his foot on the bomb also wants money.
Five rouble divided by thirty-three is... let me think... let me
think... let me think...

The BOY *calculates 5 divided by 33 is 0.151515 on the
blackboard. He can already count after the decimal point
and is very proud of his ability.*

GIRL. That is not so much per terrorist...

BOY. But maybe not every terrorist wants money. Perhaps
some only want peace, otherwise they will kill us.
Imagine: fifteen of the thirty-three terrorists want money.
Then it is five divided by fifteen and that's... let me think...
let me think...

Oh, no I do not need to calculate. Thirty-three minus fifteen is eighteen. There are eighteen terrorists who will murder us unless they get peace. That means that per terrorist... one thousand one hundred and thirty-nine divided by –

GIRL. It is now one thousand one hundred and thirty-eight.

BOY (*a little annoyed*). Well, one thousand one hundred and thirty-eight divided by fifteen... no, one thousand one hundred and thirty-eight divided by eighteen is... I can't think...

He throws his chalk away and angrily turns away from the board with the calculations.

GIRL. See. I told you: it's very complicated...

BOY. It is an unsolvable question.

GIRL. An unsolvable problem.

The GIRL *faints.*

BOY. It's a little bit warm.

The GIRL *regains consciousness.*

GIRL. Here I am.
I have a dry throat.
Do you have to go yet?

BOY. No, you?

GIRL. Are you sure?

BOY. Yes.

GIRL. Shall I push on your belly?

BOY. NO!

GIRL. It's so hot.

The GIRL *pulls off her T-shirt.*

The GIRL *faints again.*

BOY. It is warm.
I haven't been to the toilet for thirty-eight hours and twelve minutes. My previous record was thirteen hours and six

minutes. That was when I was camping with my cousins. I thus have improved my previous record by one hundred and ninety-one per cent.

Carefully he looks at the GIRL *lying unconscious on the ground. When he is sure that she sees nothing, he carefully loosens his sweater. It feels great. Carefully he takes it off more and more – until he bares his torso. He squeamishly holds his sweater in front of his bare chest.*

Lovely...

The GIRL *revives and the* BOY *quickly puts his sweater back on. It's very difficult. In his rush he tries to squeeze his head through a sleeve.*

GIRL. Can I help?

BOY. No no, not necessary...

When the BOY *has his sweater on again his hands shoot up in the air. The* GIRL *follows. She has to cough.*

Nothing's happening. We're just sitting here.

A much-delayed echo of the song 'Oh Wonderful New Future' sounds softly through the speakers. The BOY *and the* GIRL *cannot keep their hands in the air. Slowly their arms lower down. When the* BOY's *hands reach his nose, he starts to pick. Suddenly he jumps up; something is happening in the gymnasium...*

The changing of the guard.

GIRL. Two hours later.

BOY. Two hours. One thousand one hundred and thirty-seven.

GIRL. Every time another terrorist.

BOY *and* GIRL. One thousand one hundred and thirty-four.

The BOY *and* GIRL *look startled.*

One thousand one hundred and thirty-three.
Again.

And again.
One thousand one hundred and thirty-two.

The GIRL *starts to cough. It's hard to breathe.*

BOY. She has a dry throat.
Then she feels a tingling sensation throughout the body.

GIRL. Another two hours.

BOY. Her hands and feet go cold. Decrease in consciousness.

The GIRL *faints.*

The BOY *continues.*

One thousand one hundred and thirty-one.
(*Re: the* GIRL *fainting.*) Oh no, it's just warm. (*Very upbeat.*)
No need to worry…

*It has slowly become dark. Suddenly, a lot of steam is blown
on to the podium. The* GIRL *immediately comes round to the
sound.*

GIRL. Oh, how beautiful: clouds! I see clouds. I am flying…

*A light shines through the holes in the blackboard, where the
coat hooks were. They look like bullet holes. Rays of light
shine into the gymnasium. It looks magical.*

A giraffe!
Look look look.
A giraffe.
There is a giraffe in the gymnasium.

BOY. No there is not…

GIRL. The giraffe floats on long legs through the gymnasium.

BOY. A giraffe can't float… that's not possible.

GIRL. There's a giraffe nibbling on the bombs in the basket
hoop.

BOY. No there's not.
Not really.
No.

GIRL. There's a giraffe nibbling on the bombs.

The GIRL *faints.*

The BOY *changes guard again. The light changes. It's the next night.*

BOY. Nothing.
Changing of the guard.
Very hot.
Nothing is happening.
Except… in the leg of the terrorist.
In his calf.
Then slowly forward.
The shin.
The ankle.
The toes.

GIRL *and* BOY. Cramp occurs when the nerves that control your muscles make your muscles react inappropriately.
They give off too many signals causing too many muscle fibres to contract.
You can also get cramps when there's not enough glucose in your muscle because you've had too little to eat.
Cramps can also occur because the blood supply to the muscle is closed by an incorrect posture or…

The BOY *takes the balloon that is attached to the block and bursts it. The wires collapse to the floor.*

The theme from Mission: Impossible *plays. The music lowers when the* GIRL *starts talking.*

GIRL. BAM! The ceiling has come down.
The terrorist is blown to bits.
He is lying in pieces on the floor next to the ceiling.
Immediately after the explosion, the army's Special Forces – perfectly trained for their mission – storm inside through the windows. One of the heroes has steel-blue eyes and a strong-willed chin. He looks up at the leader of the terrorists who is still busy trying to load his gun, but it's too late. The hero shoots him dead.

Immediately he takes two small children under his arm and fights his way back to the window. There he puts the children to safety, to return immediately to save the others.
But it does not take long. With his great training and his precision weapons he has the terrorists eliminated in a few minutes. Then it's all over.

The Mission: Impossible *theme stops.*

Sad music begins. The BOY *holds the* GIRL *protectively while they watch the havoc in the gymnasium. The* GIRL *is crying.*

BOY. But it didn't go like that.
    The ceiling fell down.
    The bomb exploded and the terrorist blew apart.
    For a moment you can't see anything.
    Hear nothing.
    A thick mist fills the gymnasium.
    After a few minutes the smoke moves away from the wrecked windows.
    Hundreds of corpses lie on the floor.
    Mummies, daddies (not so many), grandmothers, children and terrorists.
    All dead.
    In the corner a girl with her arms around her mother's neck... both dead.
    A grandmother bent over... dead... with a toddler on her lap... dead.

GIRL. The giraffe, also dead.

The sad music stops. The gospel song 'Oh Happy Day' starts. The GIRL *and* BOY *stand up – cheerful.*

But that didn't happen either. The ceiling did come crashing down. There is smoke. That too, but when it has lifted, everyone is still alive. Puzzled, bewildered. The terrorists seem petrified. Until the leader of the terrorists slowly takes of his mask and his teary eyes become visible. He throws his weapon away and falls to his knees. He is crying.

'I'm so sorry, please excuse me, I beg your pardon. Forgive
me. This is not the right way.'
Now all the terrorists throw their weapons away, they all fall
to their knees and beg for forgiveness.
The mothers get up, wipe the dust off their clothes and look
at the terrorists in a way that only mothers can look. With a
voice full of love, they say, 'It does not matter. We forgive
you. The important thing is that you admit to your mistake.
Everyone makes mistakes. Making mistakes is easy.
Admitting your mistakes is the hard part and you managed to
do that. Bravo and a big fat thumbs up.'

'Oh Happy Day' finishes.

BOY. The ceiling has come crashing down.
Lying in the middle of the gymnasium is a large chunk
of debris.
To the right under the rubble a foot sticks out and on top you
see a lock of hair.

GIRL. That's me.
I can't hear anything. No pops. I don't feel the bombs
detonating. I do smell gunpowder, dust and the very slight
smell of a cigarette.
That's from a group of men waiting for a pause in the hail of
bullets before entering the gymnasium. The cigarette smoke
fluttered in through the shot-up window, and went up my nose.
Then the smell disappears.

*The GIRL walks to the front of the stage and picks up a chair
that has fallen over during the first explosion. Carefully she
steps on to the chair.*

I get on to the giraffe's back and we wobble through the
space to the broken window. Carefully the giraffe places two
front paws on the window sill. He bends his long elegant
legs, takes off and jumps through the window. We fly up to
the blue sky with an occasional cloud here and there.

*The GIRL gets off the chair and begins to wipe everything off
the blackboard at the back of the stage while the BOY talks.*

BOY. I look at the ceiling.
>Then I wake up in hospital.
>Beside my bed my mother is crying: 'Oh my son, oh my son, my baby. You're awake.'
>Embarrassed I turn my head the other way.
>In the afternoon I get a visit from a star footballer.
>He cries when he sees me.
>The star player goes round all the children and gives each child fifteen thousand roubles, including me.
>He gives the parents who have lost a child, twenty thousand roubles. My parents get nothing, because I'm still alive.
>For fifteen thousand roubles, I can buy three Wiis or one point five PlayStation or eight skateboards or fourteen mobile phones or four iPods.

While the BOY *cheerfully lists what he can buy with fifteen thousand roubles, the* GIRL *writes the* BOY*'s wish list on the blackboard.*

GIRL (*the* BOY *joins in occasionally with some of the below*).
>Men raise the piece of concrete beneath covering my body.
>It's too heavy. A fourth joins in. And a fifth. It works.
>My body is placed on a stretcher and carried outside.
>My head has fallen to one side
>A little bit of blood is trickling from my ear.
>I've always wanted to be on TV.

BOY. That's true, she has always said so.

The GIRL *and the* BOY *trace the entire trail that the stretcher travelled. The* BOY *pretends to be the cameraman who films everything and the* GIRL *looks proudly at the camera to see if everything is filmed the right way.*

GIRL. When the stretcher comes through the window, the lens of a camera at the side of the road finds me.
>It follows me around while I am being carried past a group of smokers.
>By the road we have to stop because of a car passing.
>A small man gestures strenuously that we need to go to a waiting car. Just before we get to the car I pass a few crying women who are comforting each other. A woman

sneezes and turns her head towards my stretcher.
Then I disappear into the car and out of reach of the
camera lens.
The cameraman sends the two minutes he has of me to the
satellite vehicle that sends the images on to the capital.
There, someone cuts out the smoking men and the passing
car. The woman who sneezes now seems to break with grief
when I pass her.
It has become a very nice story.
That story gets sent all around the world through five satellites.
Exactly fifty-one minutes and thirty-six seconds after the
camera filmed my body for the first time I appear on
television in one hundred and forty countries.

The GIRL *gets back on to the chair right in front of the
audience.*

The BOY *climbs upon the chair beside the* GIRL. *Slowly, the
stage lights switch off until only a little light is left shining on
the* BOY *and* GIRL *standing together on the chair very close
to the audience. It is a very intimate final image. He holds her.*

BOY. One hundred and forty-three countries.
    In China they play this music with it.

Music plays.

    In France, Chopin.
    In America –

Music plays.

GIRL. I'm on the television in America –

BOY. Hollywood.

GIRL. There they will interrupt the broadcasting especially
    for me. Here it takes four minutes, because everything is
    in slow motion.
    My face to one side…
    …A little bit of blood running from my ear.

The BOY *traces the path of the blood across the* GIRL*'s face.*

    It's a pity though…

BOY. What's a pity?

GIRL. That it was only that side.
This side is much nicer.

The BOY *looks extensively at the two sides of her face.*

BOY. Yes that is true…

Blackout.

The End.

A Nick Hern Book

Us/Them first published in Great Britain as a paperback original in 2017 by Nick Hern Books Limited, The Glasshouse, 49a Goldhawk Road, London W12 8QP, in association with BRONKS and Richard Jordan Productions

Us/Them copyright © 2017 Carly Wijs

Carly Wijs has asserted her right to be identified as the author of this work

Cover photograph by Murdo MacLeod

Designed and typeset by Nick Hern Books, London
Printed and bound in Great Britain by CPI Books (UK) Ltd

A CIP catalogue record for this book is available from the British Library

ISBN   978 1 84842 645 0

MIX
Paper from
responsible sources
FSC® C013604

Annie Baker
THE FLICK

Mike Bartlett
BULL
GAME
AN INTERVENTION
KING CHARLES III
WILD

Jez Butterworth
JERUSALEM
JEZ BUTTERWORTH PLAYS: ONE
MOJO
THE NIGHT HERON
PARLOUR SONG
THE RIVER
THE WINTERLING

Caryl Churchill
BLUE HEART
CHURCHILL PLAYS: THREE
CHURCHILL PLAYS: FOUR
CHURCHILL: SHORTS
CLOUD NINE
DING DONG THE WICKED
A DREAM PLAY *after* Strindberg
DRUNK ENOUGH TO SAY
    I LOVE YOU?
ESCAPED ALONE
FAR AWAY
HERE WE GO
HOTEL
ICECREAM
LIGHT SHINING IN
    BUCKINGHAMSHIRE
LOVE AND INFORMATION
MAD FOREST
A NUMBER
PIGS AND DOGS
SEVEN JEWISH CHILDREN
THE SKRIKER
THIS IS A CHAIR
THYESTES *after* Seneca
TRAPS

Phil Davies
FIREBIRD

Vivienne Franzmann
MOGADISHU
PESTS
THE WITNESS

James Fritz
THE FALL
ROSS & RACHEL

Sam Holcroft
COCKROACH
DANCING BEARS
EDGAR & ANNABEL
PINK
RULES FOR LIVING
THE WARDROBE
WHILE YOU LIE

Anna Jordan
CHICKEN SHOP
FREAK
YEN

Lucy Kirkwood
BEAUTY AND THE BEAST
    with Katie Mitchell
BLOODY WIMMIN
THE CHILDREN
CHIMERICA
HEDDA *after* Ibsen
IT FELT EMPTY WHEN THE
    HEART WENT AT FIRST BUT
IT IS ALRIGHT NOW
KIRKWOOD PLAYS: ONE
NSFW
TINDERBOX

Evan Placey
CONSENSUAL
GIRLS LIKE THAT
GIRLS LIKE THAT & OTHER PLAYS
    FOR TEENAGERS
PRONOUN

Jack Thorne
2ND MAY 1997
BUNNY
BURYING YOUR BROTHER IN
    THE PAVEMENT
HOPE
JACK THORNE PLAYS: ONE
LET THE RIGHT ONE IN
    after John Ajvide Lindqvist
MYDIDAE
THE SOLID LIFE OF SUGAR WATER
STACY & FANNY AND FAGGOT
WHEN YOU CURE ME

Phoebe Waller-Bridge
FLEABAG

Enda Walsh
ARLINGTON
BALLYTURK
BEDBOUND & MISTERMAN
DELIRIUM
DISCO PIGS & SUCKING DUBLIN
ENDA WALSH PLAYS: ONE
ENDA WALSH PLAYS: TWO
LAZARUS *with* David Bowie
MISTERMAN
THE NEW ELECTRIC BALLROOM
ONCE
PENELOPE
THE SMALL THINGS
ROALD DAHL'S THE TWITS
THE WALWORTH FARCE

Tom Wells
BROKEN BISCUITS
FOLK
JUMPERS FOR GOALPOSTS
THE KITCHEN SINK
ME, AS A PENGUIN